Glimmers

Kelsey Knott

BookLeaf
Publishing

India | USA | UK

Presentation by *BookLeaf Publishing*

Web: www.bookleafpub.com

E-mail: info@bookleafpub.com

ISBN: 9789358317138

First edition 2023

DEDICATION

To all those who lost their sight for glimmers

may you always find your way back

and make life a little more glimmery each day

ACKNOWLEDGEMENT

To my colleagues:
Thank you for inspiring me to live beyond my self-imposed limits.

To my lifelong friends:
Thank you for cheering me on, keeping me in your corner, and modeling the parts of life I'm not ready for yet. :)

To my family:
Thank you for molding my most glimmery memories, living in my heart always.

To Blake Knott:
Thank you for loving me the loudest, no matter if dust or glitter surrounds us.

PREFACE

In a society of ever-growing technology and change, it is important for me to write this book as a testament that humans are meant to create. The topic of glimmers, which LCSW psychotherapist and author Deb Dana identifies as the opposite of triggers, came to mind easily, as we all work to navigate a world moving faster than we can.

I've always known I wanted to write a book, and as a language arts teacher working to mold a new generation of creators and communicators, I knew that now was my moment to explore the value of creativity in a life that can dim it.

The process and research for this book, much like glimmers themselves, came from random daily magical moments--inspiring joyful feelings, reigniting future possibilities, and transporting me back to my most vivid memories. Through the challenges that came with getting words on pages under tight deadlines, also came a newfound appreciation for making art for the sake of art--imperfectly capturing the joys we just might miss when blinded by and bombarded with problems, first-world or not.

Here's to the micro-moments of joy that we earn simply by being human.

front porch swing

A front porch swing sways
gently in the wind
in a town you've never heard of

trees block the road
the army keeping safe
my fortress
an unfailing shield

against fast moving cars
in a hurry
to go
nowhere

listen closely
wind chimes sing the
tune of the breeze
challenging this playlist

of dreaming big
and skipping town
a red iPod nano
ignores this scene

keeping me company
a patient, half-read book
a journal stashed with sonnets
and of course the familiar swing

glides forward
freeing fears of the future

it flies back
forgiving past failures

dreams built
on this porch
didn't die here
still a faint flickering flame

the new family raises two sisters
who I hope learn
the solace
of a front porch swing

I look back and know
peace still lives there

my happy place
my childhood home

Grandma

She was a woman with an old white paring knife in hand
the one that had become her favorite
despite its need to be sharpened
You'd find her brewing coffee
that she prepped in the maker the night before
On mornings or afternoons she'd
sneak away from the kitchen
to read and watch game shows if her husband left
for an early start on the farm
She told on herself like a guilty child
when the chili had more than "just a pinch" of sugar
after everyone had already dove into their bowls
a giggle and gleaming grin followed
She strode out to her flower beds when the house was
handled
Watering, whispering, wondering
The smallest plate you've ever seen is hers
so she solidifies that her family is fed first and well
slicing pizza in half and half and half again
before pressing us to do the puzzle
proudly strewn across the card table
pretending like all the pieces are there
The world now is not the one she knew
but she still waits in its wonder contently
gracefully gathering its sweet glimmers
Together we lay back in the pile of leaves
And how grateful I am that ninety is just a number
and that the women who raised me remain magic

10/13/23

4

even the clouds covering
the sun
are captivated by its light
enough–
enchanted
by the early hours

they let through a
line of light
floating on the horizon
like a lone laser
lateral lightning

see it glisten
in its glittery glory
as if to say
magic has always lived here
why did you stop looking?

magic makers

On Halloween night
I waited and waited and waited
for the trick-or-treaters
to take their treacherous trek
toward me
and I'd fill their buckets to the brim
and give them my best guess
on their ghoulish or ghostly
or girly or glamourous costumes

but the sidewalk ended
just short of my house
neighbors might not risk
crossing a busy highway
or hop in their cars
on a holiday meant for walking
and wandering down
small town streets

yet how could it stop my parents
from fabricating just a moment
of magic
for us?

how long can you watch
your daughters' patient,
anxious eyes
awaiting joy
before you must
make the memory?

the knock
so sudden
startling my sister and I
our eyes locked
with a look that said
it wasn't in our heads

another knock
a peek through the window
proved we had patrons
mom! dad! they're here!
we reach above us
to welcome them
with an open door
we grabbed the prized bowl
of candy untouched by
anyone not under our roof
and it would stay that way

the nerves and giggles
behind the opening door
soon shifted into deep belly laughs
as we realized our guests
weren't guests at all
trick or treat!
grinning from behind
makeshift masks and
whatever getup they found in our garage

they wore this armor of junk
righteously
for the sake of
silly special moments
my own magic makers

it's always ranked low

on my list of favorite holidays
and on theirs too
but how could it stop them
from making just a moment
of magic
for us?

if you can't trust a memory

someone told me once
that we can't trust our memories
at least not exactly the way we remember them

if you can't trust a memory
why does seeing
an old cane
hanging on the coat tree
elicit echoes of it
banging against wooden bleachers
willing the home team to win?

if you can't trust a memory
why does lying
in a wide hammock
where sunlight whispers softly through the
leaves of the old trees above us
grant me his goofy grin and giggle
like he never left?

if you can't trust a memory
why does the taste of blackberries
bring me back behind the barn
braving the bristles and bushes
for a bounty we beamed about
regardless of how many
ever really made it
back to the kitchen?

if you can't trust a memory
why does the smell of saltwater and sea

transport me to our first beach trip together
when you couldn't wait to show me how
the ocean went on and on and on
as far as we could see?

if you can't trust a memory
why does how great thou art
wreck me inside
wring out my heart and catch my throat
without the casket too?

winter dreaming

snow glimmers
outside the bay window
curtained by frost
twinkling reflections
of the tall thin
ribbon wrapped
tree
a truest tribute
to the cozy simple life
I've always wanted
a rowdy
rescue dog
that I said I'd never get
is finally at ease enough to
curl up cozily
against the blanket we share
she warms me like the
flames in the fireplace
crackling and conjuring
wintry dreams
through the
black coffee steam
veiling it's luster–
the cat crawls up close
taking a break from mischief
snoozing soundly
in this dreamy scene
so serene
capturing life's fantasy

love, auntie kels

little one
you timed your presence
perfectly
we heard the news today
how ready we are
to jump into
this new chapter
it's an honor
to be a part of
your village
I can't wait to show you
how calming
a front porch swing
can be
we'll run barefoot
in the grass together
I'll pretend to like Halloween
if it makes magic for you
let me lead
glimmers to you
so you grow up to be hopeful
and work for a world
with glimmers galore
gifting generational
joy

horses

the pencil
outline of a horse
sketched
by my grandfather
past his usual
break for cigarettes
just because
it made me smile
when he captured their
essence so
perfectly
on the page

his letters
to my grandmother
catch your heart in a way
that only buried feelings
splayed on the page
a burst open heart
in written word form
from a man who
didn't say much can

when I drive by
Kentucky horse farms
I remember a man
who respected the
raw rural beauty
of the world
capturing and
collecting it

wherever he could–
but mostly,
right around home

rain grasping

the first time
I heard rainfall
on the tin roof
safe under the
patio of
our first home
I didn't even realize
how long I had
tried to manifest
this exact life

now every time it rains
I'm drawn outside
entranced by
the chance
to be allured by
such glimmering highs
to carry me
along in case
the next one
takes its time
like the rain
gliding gingerly
down the grass

how long was I in there?

when I started writing again
I materialized

I hadn't felt real
in ages

how much easier
it was to
respect myself
care for myself
companion myself
when I remembered

how being here feels
too big to handle sometimes

and spilling life
on a page
mends my most
broken corners

it's so nice
to once again
be a friend
to myself

dream team

16

how many worries were willed
into existence
and problems invented
and deadlines delusionally decided

just to find out

all you had to do
was be a teammate
to yourself

cheer yourself on
motivate and inspire
yourself
when success is upon you
or defeat for certain
treat yourself for
hard work
and rest well and
trust your intuition
for real

what could you hope for
the moment you finally decide to be
on your own team?

my heroes

two-year old me
stopped my birthday party
to read each book

gifted to me
by loved ones who
somehow already knew my heart

was somewhere beyond
the present moment–
the page my way to the world

five-year old me
was enchanted by
lightning bugs in jars

glimmers of magic
floating right before
her eyes

like the
real world
she believed in

twelve-year old me
sensed that true love
must always be right around the corner

she fell hard

when she could
no time to waste

nanny always said
don't date anyone
you wouldn't want to marry

seventeen-year old me
knew the city would soon be hers
a glimmering skyline

summoning her spirit
toward freedom and
anonymity

and home would be
where her heart was
again

twenty-two year old me
lept wide-eyed
into every grown-up part of life

at once
living too fast and large
to spot the

simple little luxuries
living just past

her lenses

twenty-five year old me
wondered when her eyes
lost the twinkle

that could catch a glimpse
of the world's wonder–
no longer second nature

she had to become
the light
she was searching for

twenty-eight year old me
finally decided
to love herself

for who she's always been
and who she knows
she can become

cheers to our past selves
these past versions
heroes

for leaping in–
no matter what lessons must be learned

contentment

a slow morning
and a steaming
cup of coffee
entrances me
sunshine
on the inside

sunlight
streams in
through emerald
curtains
my surest peace
stirred up
in still moments

I breathe in
this scene
slowly saving
my sanity

let's clink our coffee cups

cheers
to change
to goals met
to clearer paths
to versions of ourselves
that we can
believe in again

sugared strawberries

nanny's house
was a cozy
little slice
of the country

a warm glass pitcher
of sweet tea
ever-adorning the counter
reflecting the sun–
my favorite
stained-glass window

sugared strawberries
were our snack of choice
better than
my favorite
candy

together we
let television
be our excuse
for staying up
giggling and gabbing
well past
midnight
when really we
just couldn't get
enough time
together

a strong woman

with a stronger mouth
made for building character
she raised us all
whether we were hers
or not
her instincts
sharp
her heart
understanding
her intentions
love

I cried when I realized
she couldn't come
see me shiny
in my prom dress
and so
she'd never see me
toss a cap through cheers
or wear a white dress blurred by tears

living out the best parts of life
just to tell her all about it

her wise words
savvy shadows–
they follow me now

and sugared strawberries
bring her back
every time

daybreak

when the world's not awake yet
I'm sung out of my slumber
by the sighs and snores
of the four-legged friend
intersecting the king bed
she made us get

the living room rug
greets me for stretching
(and cracking and popping)
on the floor
I will my body to believe
that today is our day

I write to my future self–
how I hope she'll feel
at the end of another
long day
taking care
of children
bell to bell

I jot three
grateful thoughts
before breathing in
beliefs about today
that make moving forward worth it
and breathing out
myths my mind has already
begun to feed me

into the world I go
wearing the brave mask
rescuing it
in the
only way I know how
sacrificing
for a future to believe in

I recall
my lifelong allies
saving the world with their own
magic–
through flowers frozen for
the memories we clutch
through frames found in
familiar homes, uncovered beauty
through fun-filled times hosted
by the friend who unfailingly feels like home
through offspring fearless
like their mother once was

we're strung together
like telephone wires
faithfully following
and finding
enchantment

how lovely it is
to be inspired by
chosen family

and how noble
the pursuit
of the world's beauty
despite how it's
burned us

some days
at dusk
I am disappointed that
who I was at daybreak
had the highest hopes
for me

why couldn't she remember
this broken bird
fluttering back from flawed flocks

why must she grasp so eagerly for these
glimmering gifts
life won't grant her easily

but hope is the thing with feathers, they say
so my songbird keeps singing
for stifled souls, shattering loud silences

for Blake

where do I begin
to describe the light
that glows inside me
at the end of the day
when we're finally
safe in our first home
(not counting that
snug 500 square feet)
dwelling in the city
of my dreams

it's the same as
the light
in the stars
that twinkled
above us
years ago–
taking chances
and making promises
(too young, they said)

your loyalty
like the lingering
luster of
lightning bugs
floating closely by
quick flashes
decorating
my dark pieces
so I never forget
the warmth

of your
unwavering
love

I envy how you so
effortlessly
find fondness
for the flaws of others
a lover of life, and
everyone's cheerleader
you connect with strangers
like the familiar long-lost friend
they've anxiously awaited

you may find him
telling stories
humming tunes
plucking strings
taking jokes
working crowds
making the ordinary
exciting, and
harnessing joy
where it was once invisible

I imagine
laughing in your lap
as the glowing fireplace
illuminates what we've built
together–flames dancing
the way we do
when the world's weight
is too heavy
and moving with you
is all that feels real

rushing home on
Thursday afternoons
blasting music
singing at the top of my lungs
because our home
awaits us–
the peace
we live for

even today
I still feel like two kids
who see the world
as only opportunities
if they give enough
of themselves to
all the right places

I can't wait to share
the timeless
song of our life
and all of our tomorrows
where beauty is never promised
and the ugly ever-survivable
because of you

cleansed

29

when it rains
I leave behind my umbrella
and feel alive

present

the waves
remind me that
tomorrow's
loneliness
is not today

to my sister

when you look up to your younger sister,
there's no idea she can't talk you into:
midnight snacking, shopping sprees, dance parties
the groom to her bride; her sidekick for life

heal me with the laugh I've known a lifetime
my fiercely loyal, forever fun friend
with unmatched taste and unrivaled drive, she
earns those bubble baths, my self-care queen

our souls share memories and and truths and dreams
singing songs we first heard on a boombox
somehow we are always children again–
two kids treading tumultuous waters

if I wandered through this world without her,
where would I await radiant glimmers?

candlelight

32

crimson candles
crackle
circling ceilings
creating contentment
commemorating campfires
calmy calling
curses crowding
consciousness
crushing cares
casting conjured
clouds
concocted concerns
careening
celestially

gifts that keep giving

can you count
glimmers wriggling
their way into
your world

both
surprising
and expected

like how
the clouds take shape
for the smile you needed

or how
the place where their memory lives
rustles up their spirit nearby

or how
the mortals make magic
from moments so simple

randomly
and beautifully
anticipated
scattered

poetry

you might
just miss them
if you let the world
grind you down

if you become
a victim
to its bullshit

furnishing
the empty
flat of your heart
with fears
fueling fights
and frozen dread
so you fawn
your way
to safety

forgetting
that life's
little laughs
and
long lines of
love
linger on–
lighting

our path
to the joyful
tomorrows
we always
deserved